HEDGING
HURRICANES

A Concise Guide to Reinsurance,
Catastrophe Bonds, and
Insurance-Linked Funds

ADAM ALVAREZ

Alvarez & Associates Ltd is a UK-based consultancy
that publishes InsuranceLinked.com.

First edition published as
'Investing in Hurricanes' in 2015

Second edition published in 2017

A CIP catalogue record for this book is available
from the British Library.

ISBN-13: 978-1-5398926-3-2

Design and typeset by
www.chandlerbookdesign.co.uk

Printed in Great Britain by
Createspace

CONTENTS

Foreword by Michael Millette

Insurance-linked bonds and funds have graduated from their start as a curiosity at the edge of markets to their current status as an important investment alternative for institutional investors as well as certain individual investors around the world. When the first transactions were imagined and structured nearly 20 years ago, the notion of a tradable reinsurance market that would offer investors premium returns per unit of risk and low correlation with other sectors seemed theoretically appealing. The sector has grown to nearly $70 billion of outstanding bonds, funds, and vehicles by performing on that vision. The intervening catastrophes – including 9/11 and the Katrina series of hurricanes – have made this capital market useful to the (re)insurance industry. The recent financial crisis highlighted the value of diversification to investors and has motivated capital flows into this sector.

Adam Alvarez has done the market a great service in writing and continuing to update this concise guide to the market. He provides an understandable pathway through the jargon-strewn landscape of this sector, jargon reflecting the dual parentage of the bond and reinsurance markets. He does this by starting with underlying (re)insurance concepts and only after those are clear proceeding to the intricacies of various instruments.

The discussion of insurance-linked funds is one of the first to appear in print. He devotes attention to their history and characteristics including liquidity, jurisdictions and policies. Since most investors access the market through funds rather than directly, this survey is long overdue.

The next decade is likely to bring further developments in this asset sector as (re)insurers develop their business models to take account of the availability of capital in these forms. We will look forward to continuing updates from the author to keep track of the shape of this emerging sector.

Michael Millette – 2017, New York

Michael Millette was one of the founders of the Goldman Sachs insurance-linked securities business and the global head of Structured Finance. This gives him a unique understanding of the evolution of the ILS market within the context of the broader financial system. He was at the bank from 1994 until 2015, during which time he led many of the ILS market's most significant transactions.

In 2015, Mr Millette co-founded Hudson Structured Capital Management. Hudson Structured invests in sectors with low correlations to broader markets.

Introduction

Alternative asset classes offer investors opportunities to generate returns that are weakly correlated to the debt and equity markets. Hedge funds, Real Estate Investment Trusts (REITs) and commodity funds as well as niches such as wine, art and stamp funds all promise absolute returns that are independent of the stock market. But we live in an interconnected world and experience has shown that, in stressful times, all of these strategies are affected by what is happening in the rest of the economy.

Insurance-linked funds have experienced rapid growth in recent years by successfully making the argument that catastrophe reinsurance is an asset class that is less correlated than most. Whilst a financial collapse might cause people to buy less wine, stamps or art it won't cause a hurricane, earthquake or tsunami.

Reinsurance is not complicated but it is full of jargon. This guide aims to explain the key ideas that are necessary to make an informed investment in this sector.

The first two parts outline the types of asset that an insurance-linked fund can invest in. Part one explains what reinsurance is, why it is bought and how funds can invest in it. Part two explains insurance-linked securities – newer structures that perform a similar function to reinsurance.

Part three of the guide looks at the funds themselves. There is little consistency between the strategies of insurance-linked funds. Understanding the fundamental strengths and weaknesses of each approach might make a big difference to investments when the next loss happens.

1

Reinsurance

1.1 Introduction to reinsurance

A reinsurance company insures insurance companies. Insurance companies buy reinsurance for two related reasons: as an alternative to capital and to reduce the volatility of their results.

A single building, oil rig, or board of directors can be insured by multiple insurers each of which may in turn buy reinsurance from multiple reinsurers. Reinsurers themselves buy cover called retrocession. This web of contracts, enables very large claims to be absorbed by a global network of companies.

The simplified schematic on the below shows the traditional reinsurance hierarchy. The policies that link each entity represent a promise to pay certain losses. Rating agencies such as AM Best and S&P provide a guide to each entity's ability to pay. In recent years, insurance-linked funds have been participating at every stage of the reinsurance chain.

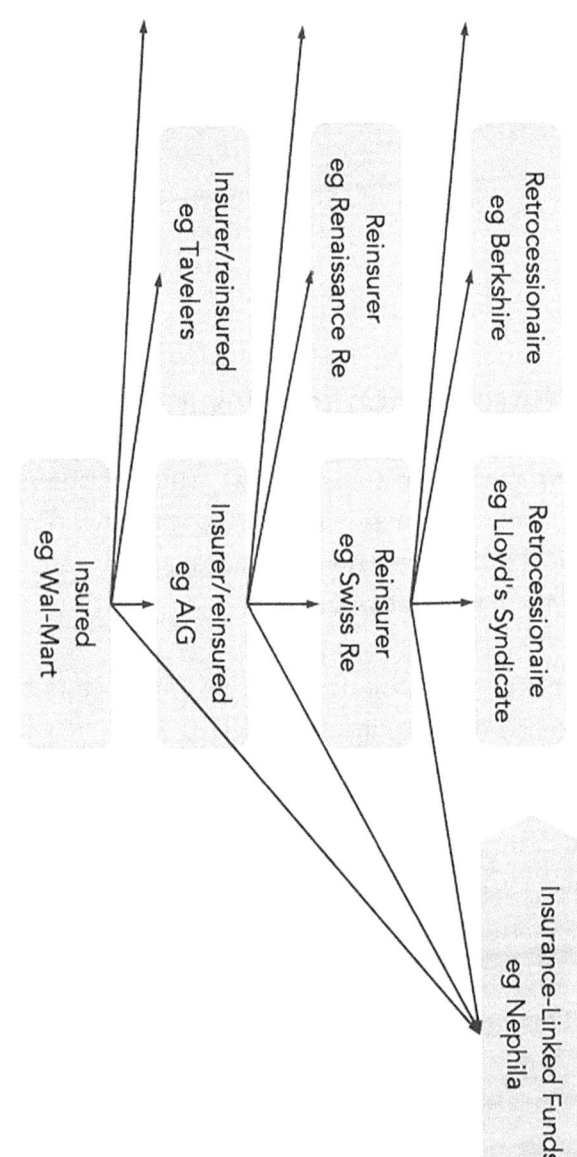

FIGURE 1 THE REINSURANCE VALUE CHAIN

Reinsurance can be broadly categorised as either excess of loss or proportional. When a reinsurer sells excess of loss reinsurance, the policy will protect the insurer against large losses helping to reduce the volatility of earnings. Whereas, when a reinsurer sells proportional reinsurance it participates in the profits and losses of the insurer (minus some fees) in a similar way to owning equity.

The reinsurance market

Swiss Re estimates that the global insurance industry collected around $4.6 trillion in premiums in 2015. Around 56% of this was life insurance and the remainder was classed as property and casualty insurance.

According to S&P, the top 40 reinsurers wrote $194 billion of net premium in 2015. Here are the largest five reinsurance groups by premium.

Company	Net reinsurance premium USD billions
Munich Re	34
Swiss Re	30
Hannover Re	16
Berkshire Hathaway Re	13
SCOR SE	13

Life insurers spent approximately 2% their premium income on reinsurance whilst property and casualty insurers spent approximately 9%.

The insurance industry spends around $25 billion on reinsurance premiums to help absorb the cost of natural disasters. It is this part of the market that has seen the majority of interest from insurance-linked funds.

Rated reinsurance

A rated reinsurer creates a diversified portfolio to minimise the probability that it will be unable to meet all of its obligations. Rating agencies review a reinsurer's business model to determine how confident they can be that the reinsurer will be able to honour all its claims. Key parameters will include the amount of capital that the reinsurer holds and the likely volatility of losses.

An A- (or better) from the rating agency AM Best is a de facto requirement for a reinsurance company. AM Best uses a quantitative model known as Best's Capital Adequacy Ratio in addition to qualitative factors to determine its rating.

The range of AM Best ratings is: A++(superior), A+, A, A-, B++, B+, B, B-, C++, C+, C, C-, D, E, F (liquidation). In practice, it is very difficult for a reinsurer to sell reinsurance if it is downgraded to below A-.

Other stakeholders in a reinsurer such as regulators and boards of directors will use different calculations to come to their own view of how much capital a rated reinsurer must hold. These may impose more or less severe constraints than the rating agencies.

Any calculation will be based on ensuring that the reinsurance company can survive an extreme stress test. But a reinsurer's theoretical liabilities are usually much greater than its capital base so an extreme, if improbable, set of events could cause the reinsurer to be unable to pay claims in full.

Fully collateralised reinsurance

Collateralised (or unrated) reinsurance is sold by reinsurers that lack credit ratings. All of the collateral that could be needed to pay claims is held in a trust account. This approach is implemented by catastrophe bonds and insurance-linked funds as it can be used to transform investments into reinsurance.

For example, a fund could sell a reinsurance contract with a maximum downside of $10m for a premium of $1m. The fund will place $9m of collateral into a trust account and the insurance company will pay $1m of premium into the same trust account. The most likely scenario is that there is no claim and at the end of the policy period the fund will take back its $9m along with the $1m of premium (an 11.1% return). If there is a full loss, the insurance company will be able to draw down $10m to help pay claims.

The creation of collateralised reinsurance has been a financial innovation that has dramatically reduced barriers to entry to the reinsurance market. A bank in Brazil or a pension fund in Canada is able to sell reinsurance policies to an insurance company in Florida or Japan using a low cost 'transformer', which converts an investment into a reinsurance transaction.

History of reinsurance

1370	First recorded reinsurance contract covering a ship sailing from Genoa to Bruges.
c1688	Opening of Lloyd's Coffee House in London which became a leading reinsurance market.
c1820	First fire reinsurance treaty in Germany.
1852	Cologne Re – the first independent reinsurance company – began writing business following the Great Fire of Hamburg in 1842.
1863	The predecessors of UBS and Credit Suisse formed Swiss Re in Zurich following a large fire in Glarus which destroyed two thirds of the town.
1880	Munich Re was established in Germany.
c1885	The first excess of loss reinsurance was sold by Cuthbert Heath at Lloyd's
1906	The San Francisco earthquake demonstrated the ability of the reinsurance market to fund catastrophic losses.
1967	Berkshire Hathaway bought National Indemnity, its first reinsurance business.
1985/86	ACE and XL were established in Bermuda.
1993	Bermuda's Class of '93 was capitalised with over $3.5 billion following Hurricane Andrew in August 1992. New reinsurance companies included Renaissance, Partner, and Tempest (now part of Chubb).
1998	Piper Alpha North Sea offshore platform disaster was one of the triggers of the 'LMX spiral' that almost caused the Lloyd's market to collapse.
2001	The Class of '01 (AWAC, Arch, Aspen, AXIS, Endurance, Montpelier and Platinum) raised more than $8 billion following the 9/11 terrorist attacks.

2005	Following hurricanes Katrina, Rita, and Wilma (and Charley, Francis Ivan, and Jeanne the year before) the reinsurance industry is recapitalised with the Class of '05. New companies including Ariel, Lancashire and Validus raised over $5 billion. In addition to this, several London Market companies followed Catlin in capitalising Bermuda based entities and investors used sidecars on a large scale to access the reinsurance market.
2011	Record losses for the reinsurance industry following a series of loss events including floods in Thailand, tornadoes in the US and earthquakes in Japan and New Zealand. No new reinsurers were established but the inflows to insurance-linked funds accelerated.
2012	Hurricane Sandy causes significant destruction in the US North East.
2015	A record 19% of property catastrophe limit is 'alternative' capital including catastrophe bonds and collateralised reinsurance.

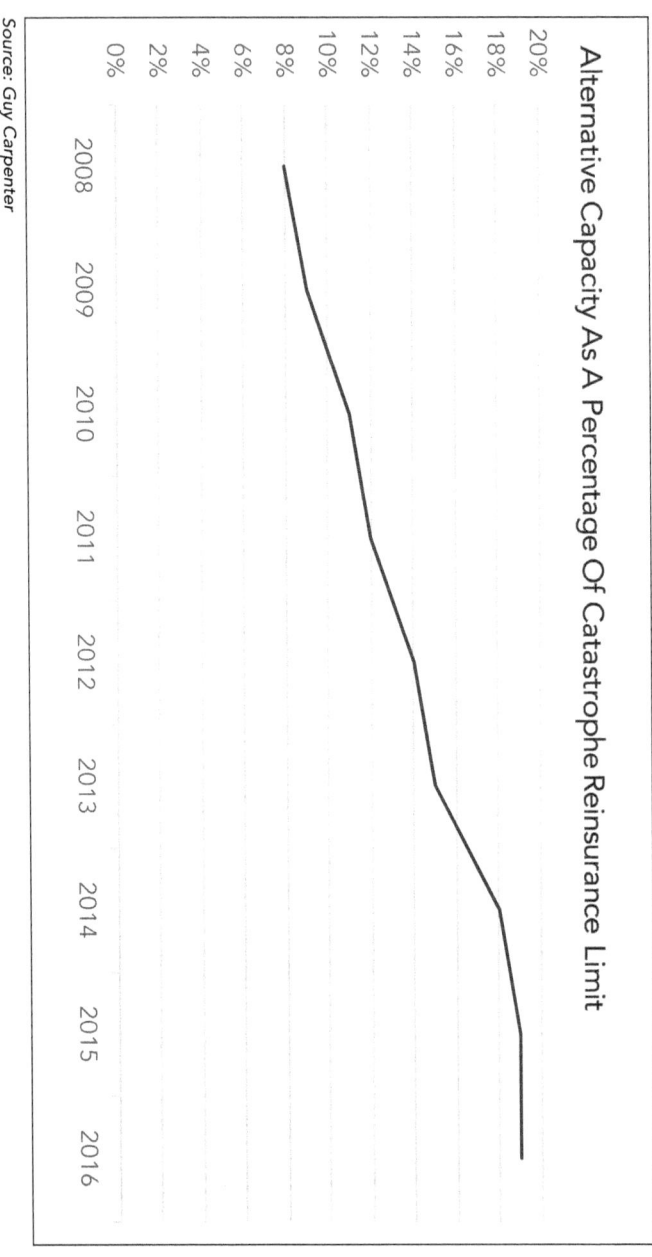

Alternative Capacity As A Percentage Of Catastrophe Reinsurance Limit

Source: Guy Carpenter

FIGURE 2 THE GROWTH OF 'ALTERNATIVE' CAPITAL

1.2 Excess of loss reinsurance

Excess of loss (XoL) reinsurance protects an insurance company against large losses that can expose its balance sheet. This is a product that has been sold by reinsurers (and retrocessionaires) for more than a century. Insurance-linked securities were developed much more recently to replicate many of the key features of XoL reinsurance. Excess of loss reinsurance and cat bonds are often used at the same time to achieve the risk management objectives of an insurance company.

An excess of loss contract can protect an insurance company from a large loss at a single location (risk excess of loss), from the accumulation of losses from a single event (catastrophe excess of loss), or the accumulation of losses during a period of time (aggregate excess of loss).

Generally, a 'programme' of excess of loss contracts is created for a single insurance company. Each 'layer' is exposed to a different level of risk in a similar way to tranches of corporate debt of differing seniority. Equivalently, an insurance company can issue a series of catastrophe bonds that consists of a number of separate securities.

The most common contract type is catastrophe excess of loss (or cat XS or cat XL or per occurrence excess of loss). This is the type of contract that has the most in common with *occurrence* catastrophe bonds. The structure is usually expressed in terms of *X* over *Y* where *Y* is the amount of loss that is necessary to trigger the contract and *X* is the limit – the maximum possible recovery.

For example, if AIG bought a $100m xs $200m cat XS policy, it would mean that AIG would be paid by the reinsurer if AIG's total claims from a single event were more than $200m. The recovery would increase proportionally with the loss so that AIG would recover zero from a $100m loss, $50m from a $250m loss, and $100m from a loss of $300m and above.

Most rated cat XL is sold with one reinstatement. This means that in the case of three $300m losses, the contract would recover $100m from the first loss, another $100m from the second loss and nothing from the third loss.

This type of reinsurance is usually sold on a UNL (Ultimate Net Loss) basis. This means that the reinsurance contract responds to the insurer's ultimate net loss, which is the actual loss paid by the insurance company. Other triggers are used in a minority of covers including Industry Loss Warranties and County Weighted Industry Loss contracts.

Industry Loss Warranties (ILWs)

Industry loss warranties are similar to excess of loss reinsurance but the contracts respond to the losses of the total industry rather than the losses of a particular company. Any figure for total industry losses will be an estimate and the contract will specify which estimate to use. In the US, the loss estimates calculated by the Property Claim Services (PCS) are usually used. Elsewhere, it is common to use the estimates provided by Swiss Re or Munich Re.

ILWs can be structured on either an aggregate or an occurrence basis, and PCS produces loss estimates for homeowners, commercial, and auto claims on a per state basis. This gives considerable flexibility in structure. For example, a $10m occurrence ILW with a €5 billion XS €10 billion European wind trigger would pay a claim of up to $10m in proportion to a single loss between €10 billion and €15 billion. Equally, a $10m ILW with an aggregate loss trigger of $20 billion would pay $10m if the total annual losses in Texas, Louisiana, Mississippi, and Alabama were greater than $20 billion.

A key advantage of ILWs is speed of execution. It is possible to sell an ILW without knowledge of the business of the protection buyer. This means that significant transactions can be agreed in a matter of hours. This ease of execution means that the ILW market has lower barriers to entry than contracts that are tied to the claims paid by a particular insurance company. The resulting supply side pressure means that ILWs often sell for a lower price than an equivalent UNL cover.

A significant disadvantage for the ILW buyer is the introduction of basis risk. This describes the mismatch between the insurance company's losses and those of the industry as a whole. For a variety of reasons, it is possible for a catastrophe to cause a relatively small loss to the industry as a whole but a disproportionately large loss to a particular insurance company (or vice versa). This is one of the reasons why ILWs make up a relatively small part of the market.

County Weighted Industry Loss (CWIL)

CWIL is a specialist product that is distributed by Guy Carpenter (other brokers have equivalent products). It was designed as a compromise between UNL and ILW type transactions. It is easier to transact than UNL cover (and so potentially cheaper) but has less basis risk than an ILW.

The trigger mechanism uses PCS to estimate the state level losses and then uses a model to allocate the losses to counties. Because the trigger is tuned to county rather than state losses, it should correspond more closely to an insurer's actual losses.

1.3 Proportional reinsurance

A proportional reinsurance contract cedes a percentage of the profit or loss from some or all of an insurer's portfolio. The simplest type of contract is a quota share, in which the percentage cession is fixed.

This type of arrangement has much in common with equity. A quota share will enable an insurer to sell more insurance policies on a fixed asset base. Often, a quota share is more flexible than raising fresh capital – they are typically renegotiated every year and can grow and shrink in line with market conditions.

Each quota share will be structured in a unique way but key terms will include:

Ceding commission – a percentage of the premium that is paid by the reinsurer to the insurer to cover the cost of sourcing the business.

Profit commission – a percentage of the profit that is paid by the reinsurer to incentivise the insurer to write profitable business. 'Deficit carry forward' means that an insurer must cover prior year losses before it can charge a profit commission on the current year (in a similar way to a high-water mark).

Occurrence or aggregate limit – the maximum loss that can be ceded to a reinsurer from one event or during the term of the deal.

In recent years, sidecars have enabled a broader range of entities to participate in proportional reinsurance. These use collateralised rather than rated structures.

1.4 Retrocession

Retrocession is simply the reinsurance of reinsurance companies. Structures have the same form as 'primary' reinsurance. Retrocession can be rated or collateralised, excess of loss or proportional.

Reinsurers' portfolios have a broad geographic scope as their clients are based across the globe. As a consequence, retrocession typically offers wide coverage. It is common for retrocession to cover losses from anywhere in the world from multiple lines of business. This breadth results in a high cost of capital for retrocessionaires which has, historically, led to high profit margins.

Retrocession has much in common with 'CDO squared' deals. Like those deals, risk has been pooled, tranched, pooled and tranched again. It is important to understand the correlations of the underlying transactions before assuming that there is a benefit to diversification.

In terms of premium, the retrocession market is significantly smaller than the reinsurance market, but the potential for high margins has meant that retrocession has proved to be an attractive part of the market for alternative reinsurers.

Pillared retrocession

A significant part of the retrocession market is now sold on a pillared basis. CATCo sells a collateralised version of this product and Everest Re sells a rated version called Purple. This is structured so that the premium is comparable to the maximum payout from a single loss, which caps the downside from individual large losses. The trade-off for this cap is that small losses are more likely and large losses are possible from multiple, medium-sized events.

2

Insurance-Linked Securities

2.1 Introduction to insurance-linked securities

Insurance-linked securities (ILS) are tradable, high-yielding debt instruments that are used by companies (usually insurance and reinsurance companies) to transfer insurance risk to the capital markets. A large majority of the ILS market is composed of property catastrophe bonds (cat bonds), which are typically used as an alternative to buying traditional catastrophe reinsurance. Other types of insurance-linked securities include mortality bonds, longevity bonds, and XXX bonds.

The securities pay periodic coupons to the investor during the life of the bonds (cat bonds typically have a three- or four-year maturity but can range from one to five years). The coupon consists of a risk-free return (often three-month treasuries) plus a spread that depends on the risk of default and market conditions at the time of issue. The principal is at risk following a trigger event (such as a hurricane or earthquake) of sufficient magnitude.

A semi-liquid secondary market exists that is facilitated by a number of specialist broker-dealers. Some of these firms issue weekly pricing sheets that include guidance on the current pricing level of outstanding bonds.

The market

As at September 2016, the total value of cat bonds on risk was $23 billion. For investors, cat bonds are attractive because their returns are largely uncorrelated with other financial markets. They have also paid higher coupons than comparably-rated corporate instruments.

Structure

Catastrophe bonds are issued by a special purpose vehicle (SPV), typically domiciled in Bermuda. The bond is placed with institutional investors through investment banks, while the SPV invests the proceeds in highly rated assets such as short-dated treasuries. The cat bond itself is issued as notes by the SPV. These notes are often given a rating by an agency, such as S&P, which will give guidance on the risk of default. The coupon that the notes pay out is funded by a combination of the 'risk-free' returns generated by the collateral, along with premiums paid by the issuer. If no trigger event occurs during the life of the bond, the SPV returns the entire principal to the investor at maturity. If the bond is triggered, the SPV liquidates the assets and pays the sponsor all, or part, of the proceeds.

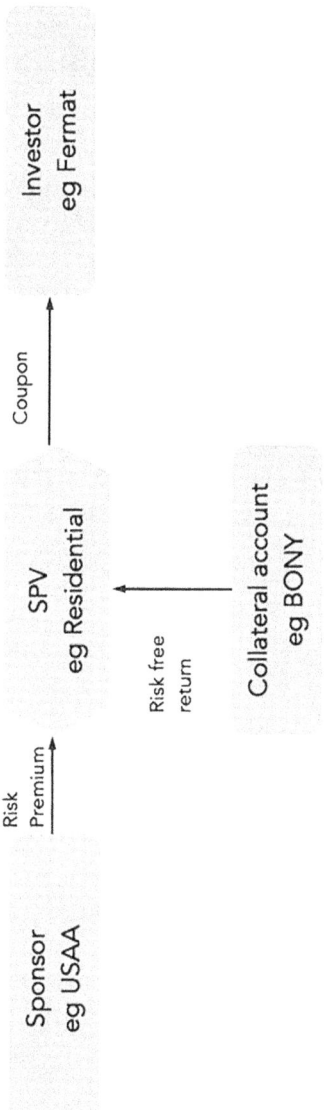

FIGURE 3 SCHEMATIC OF AN INSURANCE-LINKED SECURITY

Legal form

Most insurance-linked securities are structured to rely on rule 144A (more recently, there has been an increase in the number of 'private' cat bonds issued under Regulation D). This limits the marketing process and means that only Qualified Institutional Buyers (QIBs) with more than $100m of assets are able to invest.

History

Issuers of insurance-linked securities have maintained a steady pace of innovation since the structure was first conceived in the mid-1990s. As the asset class has become more mainstream, it has been used to hedge a growing range of risks.

1994	Hannover Re completes the first catastrophe bond.
1997	The first ILS fund – Nephila – is formed as part of the broker Willis. American Skandia issued the first life bond. Tokio Marine creates the first parametric bond.
1998	Total issuance is greater than $1 billion of bonds for the first time.
2003	Genworth issues the first 'XXX' bond. Swiss Re issues the first extreme mortality bond.
2005	The first car insurance bond is issued by AXA.
2007	Nephila issues Gamut Re – the first (and only) insurance-linked collateralised debt obligation.
2008	Four bonds that used Lehman Brothers as their LIBOR swap counterparty are impaired during the financial crisis. Subsequent bonds have been subject to much tighter collateral conditions.
2010	Aetna sponsors the first health bond and Swiss Re sponsors the first longevity bond.
2011	Tornadoes in the US and an earthquake in Japan lead to two total defaults totalling $500m.
2016	Outstanding issuance is around $23 billion.

2.2 Property catastrophe bonds

Property catastrophe bonds (cat bonds) are the largest part of the insurance-linked securities market. Insurers and reinsurers sponsor cat bonds to hedge the risk of very large losses from events such as hurricanes and earthquakes.

Investors can buy bonds on either the primary or the secondary market. The principal is at risk in the event of a catastrophe that affects the sponsoring company. Following a trigger event, the principal will be released to the sponsor to enable it to pay for financial losses (the claims it receive from its policyholders).

For sponsors, cat bonds offer an attractive alternative to standard catastrophe reinsurance for low frequency, high severity catastrophes. The benefits of cat bonds include the tenor (cat bonds are usually multiyear deals compared to annual reinsurance contracts), the security (100% of the potential liability is held in trust), and the pricing (in recent years many cat bonds have been competitively priced compared to traditional reinsurance contracts).

Structure

Cat bonds are structured to protect the sponsor from low probability, high severity events (analogous to an out-of-the-money option). Insurers pay high frequency (or attritional) losses from the premium that they receive from their policyholders. Catastrophe losses can be larger than an insurer's premium and can threaten its capital. Cat bonds can be used to reduce the capital that an insurer is required to hold by regulators and rating agencies.

Occurrence cat bonds respond to a single large event. Following a large event, either the sponsor calculates the total losses from pre-agreed lines of business or an index is calculated by a third party. If this number is greater than the attachment point, the bond will default and make a payment to the sponsor. A complete default will occur if this number is greater than the exhaustion point.

Aggregate cat bonds work in a similar way except that losses from all events in a period are aggregated. If this amount is greater than the attachment point, the bond will default.

Less common structures include bonds that pay out following two or more large events.

Triggers

Indemnity

Indemnity cat bonds are triggered by the sponsor's actual losses. For instance, a bond could cover losses of $100m in excess of $200m, meaning that the bond will be triggered if the sponsor's losses add up to more than $200m and will default in full if the sponsor's losses are greater than $300m.

In recent years, indemnity triggers have been used in increasing numbers of bonds. They are popular with sponsors due to the limited amount of basis risk. Unlike other trigger types, the payout of the bond should have a well-defined relationship to the sponsor's actual losses.

Modelled loss index

In the case of a modelled loss trigger, the losses are calculated using catastrophe models provided by companies such as AIR Worldwide, RMS, and EQECAT. When there is a large event, the event parameters are run against a model of the sponsor's exposure. The cat bond is triggered if modelled losses are greater than a certain threshold.

Industry index

Cat bonds that are indexed to industry losses are triggered when the insurance industry loss from a particular event reaches a certain threshold, such as $30 billion. The cat bond will specify which agency it will use to determine the industry loss figure, the most popular being ISO's Property Claim Services in the US and Swiss Re Sigma and PERILS AG in Europe.

Parametric index

Parametric cat bonds are triggered by a formula that uses parameters that are measurements taken from actual catastrophe events. Examples include: the strength of the

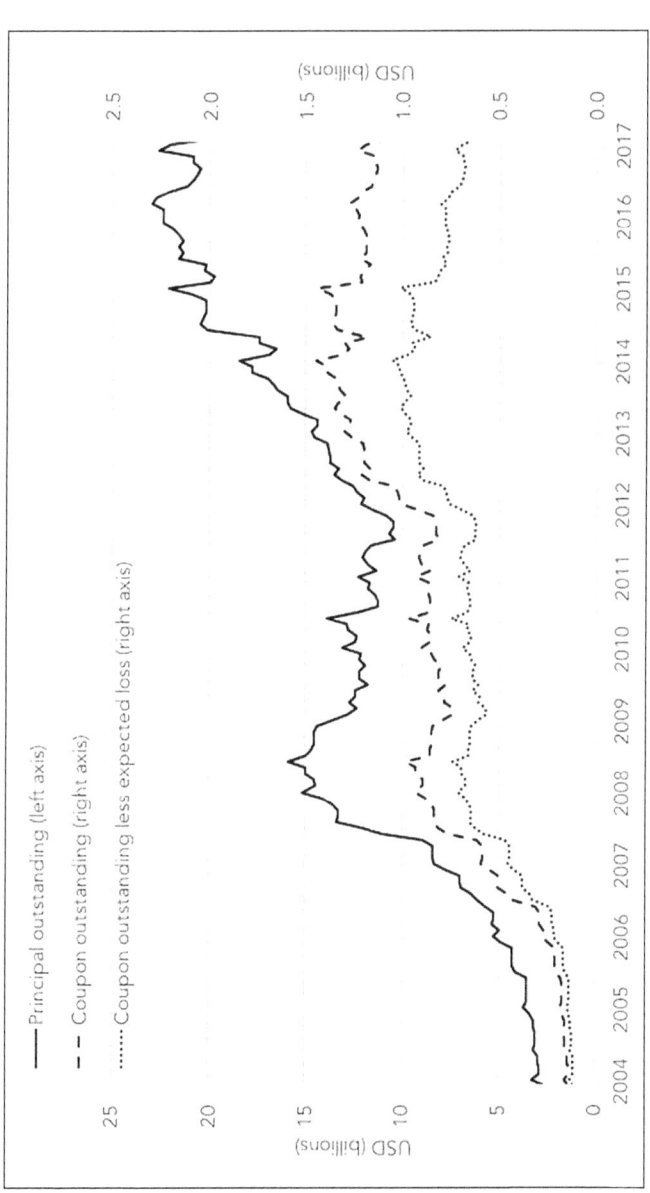

FIGURE 4 GROWTH OF THE CAT BOND MARKET

ground motion at particular measuring stations during an earthquake; wind speeds during a hurricane; or water depth during a flood. Parametric triggers are defined by third parties such as the US Geological Survey and are popular with investors due to their transparency. Another benefit is the potential for rapid payouts.

2.3 Life bonds

Life insurers and reinsurers have also made use of the insurance-linked securities market. Generally, purchasers of life insurance policies pay an unknown amount of premium for a known payout. This is the reverse of how the property insurance market works, and creates a different set of structuring challenges.

Additionally, life insurance is 'long tail' in the sense that it can take many decades to settle a life policy. This tail makes the financing of life insurance sensitive to actuarial assumptions, such as life expectancy and investment returns. Different regulatory regimes impose different assumptions, which result in various capital requirements. The various types of life bond have evolved to meet those requirements.

Mortality bonds

These types of security have the most in common with property catastrophe bonds. They protect life reinsurers from the risk that large numbers of people die earlier than expected due to some national or international event. This could be pandemics, war, or natural disasters. Regulators require life reinsurers to demonstrate that they would remain solvent in these scenarios. A mortality bond is an alternative to holding capital.

Like property catastrophe bonds, collateral is held in trust by a special purpose vehicle for three to five years and then returned to investors unless there is a trigger event. Mortality bonds have triggers that are linked to particular published mortality indices such as the US Center for Disease Control. This introduces the possibility for basis risk as the individuals covered by a particular life reinsurer may be affected more or less than the general population.

The first mortality bond, Vita 1, was issued by Swiss Re in 2003. Since then only three other sponsors have issued these types of bond: AXA, Munich Re and SCOR. Notably, all four sponsors have European regulators.

In 2012, Swiss Re sponsored Mythen Re, which was the first bond to obtain coverage against both North Atlantic hurricane and UK extreme mortality risk through a single offering.

XXX and AXXX bonds

Regulation XXX (notating the roman numeral for 30) and the actuarial guideline known as AXXX are reserve requirements set out by the National Association of Insurance Commissioners (NAIC) that affect different types of policy – term life and universal life respectively. The NAIC requirements have been in place since the beginning of 2000 and are generally thought to be overly conservative for the funding needs of these types of policy. This additional, redundant capital can reduce returns.

These reserves are often funded with letters of credit but their variable cost and availability does not match the duration of the reserves. In 2003, Glenworth securitised the first XXX bond. The bonds are characterised by long tenors (30 years or longer for AXXX bonds), low coupons, and high ratings. Often the rating was improved through a credit rating from a monoline insurance company.

Many of these securities experienced serious difficulties during the 2008 financial crisis as the collateral had been invested in mortgage-backed securities.

Embedded value bonds

Embedded value bonds can be used to turn future profits, premium income, and intangible assets into cash. These deals securitise books of life insurance business, individual life, group life, annuity, and investment life products. They provide insurers with financing to underwrite new business and free up capital to fund growth, acquisitions, or to be returned to shareholders.

Generally, these transactions involve limited risk transfer as the liabilities associated with the underlying insurance policies remain with the insurer. However, in the event of extreme mortality or premium lapses, investors may receive reduced or even no payment. In some cases, investors will assume some interest rate risk as policies can include interest rate guarantees.

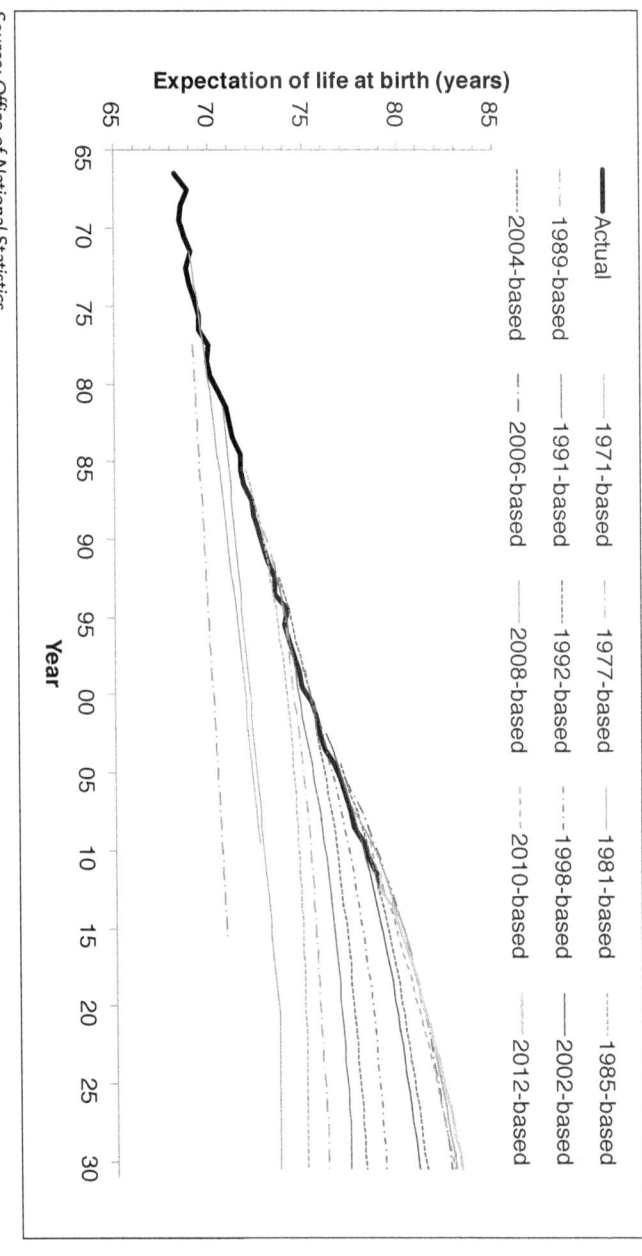

Source: Office of National Statistics

FIGURE 5 UNITED KINGDOM: PROJECTED LIFE EXPECTANCE AT BIRTH, FOR MALES, 1966-2031

2.4 Other bonds

In addition to property catastrophe bonds and life bonds, the history of the ILS market has seen the development of a number of other types of securitisation.

Longevity bonds

Pension funds face the opposite risk to life insurers – their capital is at risk in the event that their customers live significantly longer than actuarial estimates. In the past, actuaries have consistently underestimated improvements in life expectancy.

Several options are available to pension funds to hedge this risk, including owning a large life book. At the end of 2010, Swiss Re issued the $50m Kortis Capital, which protected it from the consequences of male life expectancies aged 75–85 in England and Wales improving faster than male lives aged 55–65 in the US. Swiss Re was exposed to a UK pension portfolio and a US life insurance portfolio.

Health bonds

The US health insurer Aetna has pioneered the use of ILS for hedging the volatility in its medical claims. From 2010 to 2016, the company placed $1.2 billion of bonds that trigger on Aetna's claims experience.

Other

Less common structures include Hoplon which was issued in 2011 to cover MyLotto24 from lottery payments exceeding a certain level over three years; Sparc in which Axa securitised a motor insurance portfolio; and Crystal Credit which protected Swiss Re from poor performance in its trade credit business.

Also, in 2007, Nephila used a CDO structure to sponsor Gamut Re, which sold tranched securities (equity and four bonds) on a portfolio of bonds and other instruments.

As demand for ILS continues to grow, we can expect to see structuring agents continue to bring new types of risk to the market.

3

Insurance-Linked Funds

3.1 Introduction to insurance-linked funds

Insurance-linked funds, alternative reinsurers or hybrid reinsurers, are terms that describe a variety of vehicles that sell reinsurance (and insurance and retrocession). Unlike 'traditional' reinsurers, they are designed to be capitalised in a way that is directly tied to the underlying assets and not correlated to market returns.

The possibility of diversifying returns has made these funds increasingly popular. An investor now has a large number of funds to choose from, each with its own investment strategy. There are open-ended and closed-ended funds; onshore and offshore funds; independent funds and reinsurer sponsored funds. Some funds use their large size to control terms and conditions, others use their small size to stay nimble. Some funds target well-modelled, transparent, liquid securities, while others target opaque, long-dated private deals.

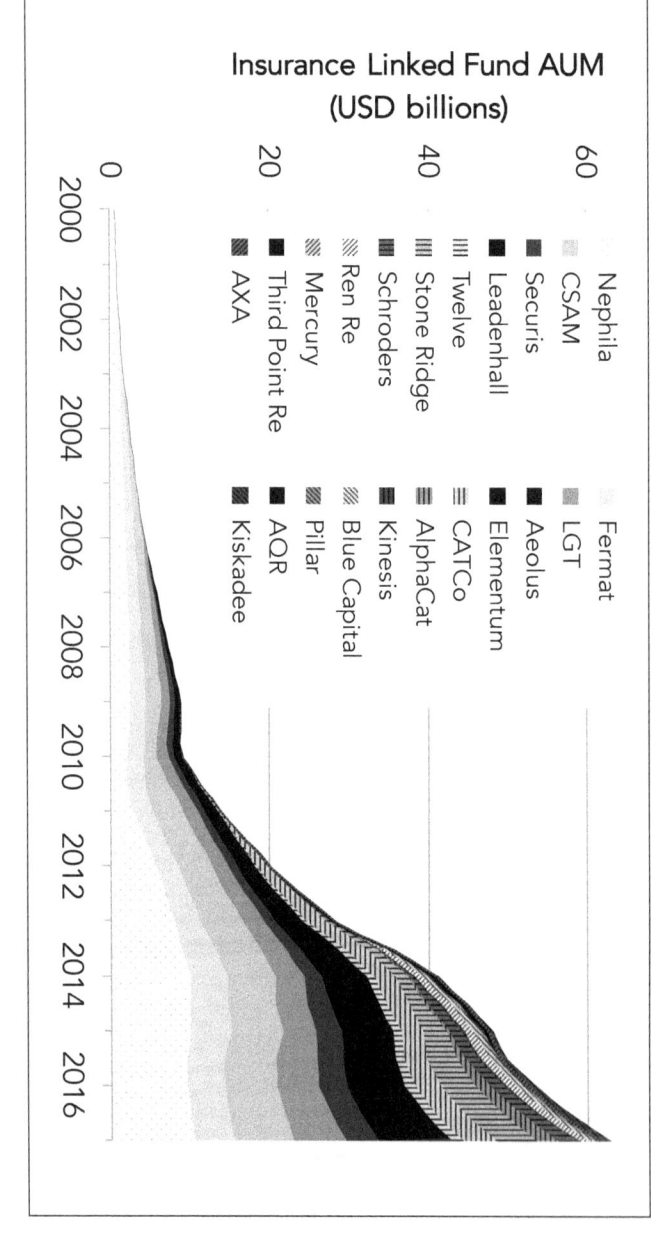

FIGURE 6 ESTIMATED GROWTH OF SOME OF THE LARGER FUND MANAGERS

Sidecars

Sidecars are another vehicle that enable investors to access insurance returns without taking market risk. They are a collateralised version of quota share reinsurance. Sidecars typically have a tenor of a few years and provide investors with the returns of all or part of a reinsurer's portfolio. Originally, they were used as crisis capital by reinsurers, but are increasingly becoming another channel for reinsurers to manage third party capital.

Sidecars typically have two types of fee – a management fee (or overider) and a performance fee (or profit commission).

One variation on the theme of sidecars is Renaissance Re's long-running, rated sidecars – DaVinci and Top Layer. These enable investors to access operational leverage, which is difficult in fully collateralised structures.

History of insurance-linked funds

1997	Just a few years after the first ILS transactions, Frank Majors and Greg Hagood formed Nephila as part of the broker Willis.
2001	Fermat became the second 'cat bond fund'.
2005	In the market dislocation following Hurricane Katrina numerous temporary sidecars are created. The collateralised retrocession specialist, Aeolus, is formed.
2008	The financial crisis vindicates much of the non-correlation argument (with the notable exception of four catastrophe bonds that default due to their suspect collateral).
2011	The first closed ended fund is listed in London by CATCo introducing a new group of investors to the asset class.
2012	The first onshore mutual fund is launched by Stone Ridge allowing US retail investors to access the market through their Regulated Investment Advisor.
2013	Numerous 'traditional' reinsurers create their own fund manager platforms. Blue Capital lists the first ILS fund on the New York Stock Exchange.

3.2 Liquidity

The mismatch in liquidity between what is demanded by many investors and the structure of the underlying instruments has been a significant obstacle in the development of insurance-linked funds. Many of the largest pension funds are used to investing in vehicles with daily, or more frequent, liquidity. Property reinsurance deals are generally one-off, annual contracts with no secondary market. When there is a potential for loss, claims can take several years to settle.

When reinsurance deals were securitised in the form of cat bonds, it became possible to trade out of a reinsurance position for the first time. Another advantage of an active secondary market was that there were now market prices for reinsurance transactions. This meant that it was possible to calculate an objective NAV for a fund, which is another requirement for many investors.

Open-ended funds

The first funds – Nephila and Fermat – were cat bond only, open-ended funds. The secondary market meant that they were able to commit to producing monthly NAVs and providing frequent liquidity. Most funds have diversified away from pure cat bond strategies though the majority maintain an open-ended structure. The introduction of less liquid assets to insurance-linked funds has become an issue that is addressed in a variety of ways.

Closed-ended funds

More recently, some insurance-linked funds have used closed-ended structures to raise capital. The simplest approach is to have an annual venture where money is raised, deployed for an underwriting year, and returned to investors as it is released from contracts. However, this forces fund managers to raise fresh capital each year.

Another approach is to create a closed-ended fund and list it on a stock exchange. There is a considerable regulatory burden associated with a public listing, but there are significant advantages. The fund manager has access to permanent capital, and investors are able to trade out of their position on the exchange.

3.3 Jurisdiction

Insurance-linked funds and their managers, have structured themselves in a variety of ways to access investors in various jurisdictions.

Bermudian funds

The most popular jurisdiction for both funds and fund management teams is Bermuda. Bermuda has been at the centre of the global reinsurance market for many years. The recapitalisation of the industry following Hurricane Andrew in 1992, the 9/11 terrorist attacks in 2001 and Hurricane Katrina in 2005 enabled the jurisdiction to build up considerable infrastructure. Its location has ensured easy access to the New York and London markets.

The local regulator – the Bermuda Monetary Authority (BMA) – has a good understanding of the reinsurance business. Recent legislation has included the creation of the Special Purpose Insurer legal structure, which has made it significantly easier to create the vehicles that are essential to many of the funds. In addition to the funds, Bermuda also hosts a variety of specialist service providers including lawyers, accountants, fund managers and transformers.

US funds

A number of insurance-linked funds are closed to US investors due to the additional regulatory burden.

But in recent years, fund managers have devised structures to access US investors.

Stone Ridge created open-ended 1940 Act mutual funds at the beginning of 2013. At the end of the same year, it raised money in an interval structure, which will allow it to access less liquid investments. Both of these funds have largely been distributed through registered investment advisors.

Also in 2013, Blue Capital established a listed fund on the New York Stock Exchange (NYSE: BCRH). This uses a corporate structure to enable investors to access reinsurance. It outsources most functions to external entities and aims to distribute 90% of distributable income. This strategy is designed to ensure that the stock trades at close to NAV and is insulated from market risk.

US based funds such as Elementum and Fermat are required to register with the SEC. Other funds such as AlphaCat have chosen to register in order to enhance their profile with investors.

European funds

Switzerland is the home of two of the largest fund managers – Credit Suisse Asset Management (CSAM) and LGT. Both funds are part of private banks and many of their clients are wealthy individuals and family offices.

A number of fund managers have taken advantage of the UK closed-ended fund structure and listed on the London Stock Exchange. The list includes CATCo, and Blue Capital. These fund managers have the advantage of permanent capital – for investors, liquidity is provided by secondary trading on the London Stock Exchange. Drawbacks for the fund manager include significant regulation and disclosure requirements.

UCITS (Undertakings for Collective Investment in Transferable Securities) is a European initiative that should allow a fund that is regulated in one jurisdiction to be 'passported' into other parts of the EU. A number of managers have UCITS funds. The list includes Secquaero, Plenum and LGT. UCITS status has a cachet that extends beyond the EU as the designation is helpful in raising funds in various other regions.

The Bermudian fund, Nephila, has established a Lloyd's Syndicate. This is a mechanism to sell rated reinsurance rather than a way to raise capital.

3.4 Nine unanswered strategy questions for insurance-linked funds

'The product warning that 'past performance does not necessarily predict future results' may be truer for insurance-linked funds than for any other asset class. The heavily skewed distributions of possible fund returns mean that, in any year, returns are unlikely to be close to the average. It would take decades – if not centuries – of performance data to differentiate between lucky portfolio managers and skilful ones.

But there are real differences between managers and funds. When insurance losses happen (and when they don't), funds perform very differently. On at least nine dimensions, insurance-linked funds pursue divergent strategies. There are good arguments for each strategy and, to an extent, different business models will suit different investors. Knowing which choices each manager has made and understanding the implications are key to making wise investment choices.

1. **Remoteness of risk.** The underlying assets in insurance-linked funds can sit at very different points on the risk-reward spectrum. *Is it better to invest in highly rated, risk-remote tranches or more 'in-the-money' layers?*

    Expected returns can be greater for high-yielding transactions but the ratio of coupon (or rate-on-line) to expected loss is often higher for deals at the lower end of the risk-reward spectrum.

2. **Diversification**. Funds have different philosophies regarding the importance of reducing the correlation of assets within their portfolios. *Is it better to select the most profitable business or to diversify by geography and peril?*

   Insurance-linked funds are inherently diversifying, and investors typically allocate less than 5% to the strategy. This makes many investors very tolerant of focused portfolios. Other investors would rather trade part of their returns for exposure to a well-diversified portfolio.

3. **Reinsurance value chain**. Insurance-linked funds participate in all stages of the insurance–reinsurance–retrocession value chain. *Is it better to protect the original insurance buyer or portfolios of portfolios of policies?*

   Funds that move close to the customer can access better data and improved transparency, while reinsurance and retrocession contracts offer the fund more flexibility and the ability to structure deals that are a better fit for collateralised reinsurance structures.

4. **Scale.** The largest managers are over 50 times bigger than the smallest ones. *Is bigger better?*

Large managers argue that their scale gives them negotiating power, while smaller ones contend that they have more opportunities because they can make material investments in more transactions.

5. **Leverage.** Some insurance-linked funds sit on cash, while others use leverage to amplify gains and losses. *How much leverage should be employed by insurance-linked funds?*

Fund returns can be leveraged in different ways. One approach is to use catastrophe bonds as collateral for bank loans. Another approach is to use the rating of a controlled vehicle or the rating of a third party fronting carriers to invest in unfunded limits.

6. **Liquidity.** Insurance-linked funds vary considerably in the liquidity they offer to investors. *How much liquidity can be promised to investors given the underlying investments?*

Most insurance and reinsurance contracts are annual, but claims – or potential claims – can lock up capital for much longer. Some funds provide the manager with permanent capital, while others offer daily liquidity.

7. **Third-party catastrophe models.** All funds use third-party models as part of the risk-evaluation process but they vary in their willingness to assume unmodelled risk. *How important is it to use third-party catastrophe models to evaluate all risks?*

Third-party catastrophe models provide a standardised way of evaluating the risk of each deal, whereas quantifying unmodelled risks requires fund managers to make highly subjective judgments – though the models themselves contain large uncertainties and provide materially different results from one another.

Many insurance risks are not modelled by the third-party vendors so avoiding unmodelled risk significantly reduces the number of investable opportunities.

8. **Reinsurer relationship.** Some fund managers are independent or owned by larger asset managers, while others are owned or partially owned by reinsurers. *What are the advantages of a close relationship with a reinsurer versus independence?*

Independent managers avoid potential conflicts with the reinsurer's balance sheet (although may still have to manage the conflicts between their various funds).

Access to business in various market conditions is important to the success of insurance-linked funds. A relationship with a reinsurer may help smaller funds see more of the market. Reinsurers can also offer their sister funds access to back office infrastructure and cheap fronting.

9. Hedging. Increasingly, funds use ILWs and other mechanisms to hedge insurance risk. *Is the downside reduction worth the reduction in expected returns?*

Most hedging strategies reduce expected returns, so investors need to decide if they are targeting a strategy that maximises returns or one that limits downside risk.

These choices are specific to insurance-linked funds, but other important strategy decisions are generic to all asset classes. These include the jurisdiction and regulatory environment; the alignment of interests and governance; and, of course, the quality of the systems and people.

3.5 Looking to the future

The success of insurance-linked funds in growing their asset bases is one reason that investors' demand for reinsurance and insurance-linked securities has significantly outpaced the supply. The current imbalance is causing considerable strain on the business models of both reinsurers and ILS funds.

In California, just 10% of homeowners buy earthquake insurance. In developing countries, insurance take-up can be much lower. An effective way to increase the supply of reinsurance would be to persuade people to buy more insurance.

Despite much talk, little progress has been made in growing the pie. In the US, overregulation and the politicisation of the industry have hampered innovation. But it also seems that insurers could do more to sell products that people want to buy.

One recent trend is 'InsurTech'. Entrepreneurs from Silicon Valley and elsewhere have come to view the insurance industry as an opportunity for the kind of disruptive innovation that has transformed industries such as publishing and music. A growing number of start-ups are attempting to create new products and distribution channels. While many of these products are genuinely innovative, it is not yet clear which of them will resonate with consumers.

The widening gap between the supply and the demand of reinsurance business is unsustainable. Sooner rather than later, either losses or lack of losses will cause some reinsurers and fund managers to falter. It is hoped that readers of this guide are now in a stronger position to judge which strategies are likely to weather the next storm.

4

Appendix

4.1 Reinsurance jargon

Basis risk

The risk of a mismatch between actual insurance losses and the trigger of the contract that has been used to hedge losses.

Expected loss (EL)

The mean loss to a contract. This is often expressed as a percentage of the limit. For example, 1% EL means that the average losses are 1% of the maximum loss.

Fronting carrier

A rated insurer or reinsurer that loans its rating to unrated (or poorly rated) reinsurers to enable them to access more types of business.

Limit

The maximum downside to a contract due to one event (occurrence limit) or during a period (aggregate limit).

Premium – written, earned, gross and net

The written premium of a portfolio of business is 100% of the premium from policies that incept in a period. The earned premium is the pro rata part of the premium that 'earns' during the period. A $100 policy that incepts on July 1 2017 would contribute $100 of written premium to 2017 or $50 of earned premium in 2017 and $50 of earned premium in 2018.

Net premium is the gross premium less the cost of reinsurance (or retrocession).

Probability of attachment

The probability that there will be some loss to the contract. This will be greater than or equal to the expected loss.

Probability of exhaustion

The probability that there will be a 100% loss to a contract. This will be less than or equal to the expected loss.

Rate on line (RoL)

The annual premium for a contract expressed as a percentage of the limit. If a contract has a maximum downside of $10m and the price is $1.5m, then the price is 15% rate on line – or just '15 on line'.

Reinstatement

A reinstatement means that after a client has recovered from a reinsurance contract, the reinsurer is obliged to sell and the client is obliged to buy cover for a second event. The most common type of catastrophe reinsurance contract is '1@100%'. This means that there is one reinstatement and that the price is 100% of the original premium. Usually they are '100% as to time', which means that the reinstatement premium is the same regardless of when the loss happens.

Transformer

A licensed insurance company that exists to enable investors without an insurance licence to sell reinsurance.

4.2 Catastrophe modelling

Models built by RMS, AIR and CoreLogic are used by most reinsurers and insurance-linked funds for pricing individual transactions and for portfolio management. These models are also an essential component of rating agency evaluations and regulatory filings. The output of catastrophe models is the probability distribution of financial loss from certain perils. This output can be used to answer important questions including:

- *What is the mean loss to a Floridian house from hurricanes each year?*

- *What is the probability that tornadoes cause more than $20 billion of damage to US homes in one year?*

- *What is the probability of default of a particular catastrophe bond?*

The input for a catastrophe model is a database that records details of all the insured property that is being analysed. This data is usually captured by the insurance company during the underwriting process and includes the location, the type of construction, what it is used for, its value and the terms of the insurance coverage.

A hurricane model (for example) will contain a description of thousands of hypothetical storms that represent the continuum of possible storms that could occur in a region.

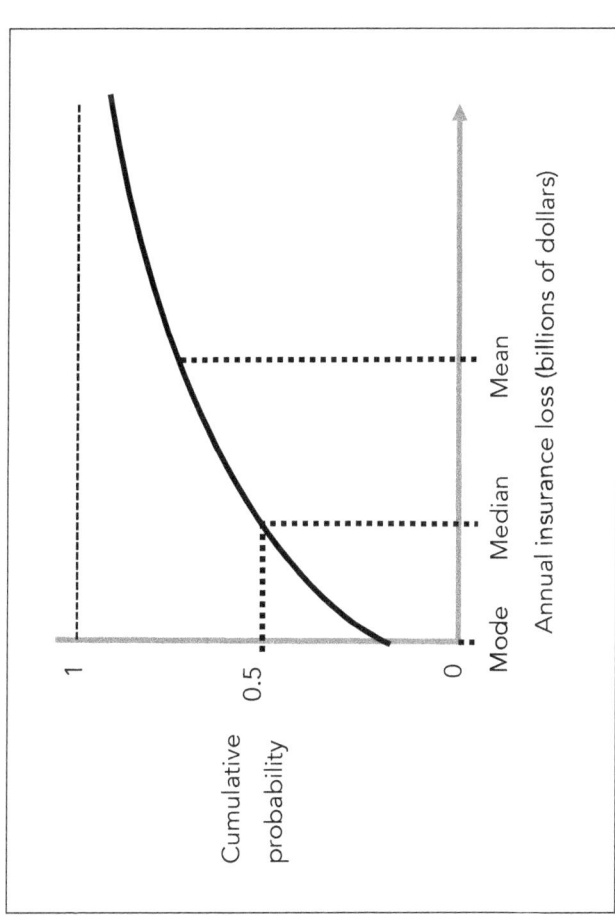

FIGURE 7 ILLUSTRATIVE OUTPUT OF A CATASTROPHE MODEL FOR US HURRICANE RISK

For each storm, the model calculates the financial loss to the properties in the exposure database.

Given the likelihood of each storm, it is then possible to calculate a probability distribution of different levels of loss.

Uncertainty

The outcome of a throwing a dice is unknowable, but the probability of getting each number is a sixth (aleatoric uncertainty). Catastrophe models also contain another, less tractable type of uncertainty. Even among experts, there is no consensus on the average number of hurricanes in a particular year (epistemic uncertainty). The challenge for catastrophe models is to calculate the value of a roll of a dice with an unknown shape.

In fact, the level of knowledge associated with the frequency of Atlantic hurricanes is high compared to other perils that reinsurers are interested in quantifying. In many parts of the world, earthquake models rely on a handful of data points and little understanding of the physical processes that drive them. For terrorism, not only is the probability of an attack extremely difficult to determine, but the risk also changes with each news cycle.

The large uncertainty in the frequency of events is just the beginning of the difficulties in building accurate catastrophe models. It is compounded by uncertainty around the size and severity of events and then by uncertainty around how a wind speed or earth motion will affect a particular building. Additionally, there is often a great deal of uncertainty about how the legal and political environment following a large disaster will affect insurance claims.

Nevertheless, in the last 15 to 20 years property insurers and reinsurers have become totally reliant on cat models for all the key pricing and capital decisions that drive their businesses. These models have also played a large role in enabling capital market investors to be comfortable with catastrophe risk.

One important reason for their success is that cat models introduce a common yardstick to measure the relative value of alternative decisions. It is often possible to say with some confidence that the risk of a deal is 10% more than the same deal last year or 20% less than some other deal. But the absolute value of risk is much harder to specify.

When making investment decisions involving hundreds of millions of dollars it is tempting to look for reassurance from a single 'accurate' model. But the reality is that quantifying the risk of infrequent natural disasters relies on making assumptions that are unknowable – either in practice or in principle.

4.3 ILS defaults

Since the creation of the ILS market in the 1990s a number of bonds have defaulted. Some of these have occurred in an orderly way as anticipated in the contractual documentation, whilst others have been more contentious. Often the circumstances of these defaults have shaped the structure of subsequent issues.

Kelvin Re (Koch Energy, 2000)

This was the first weather cat bond issued in 1999 by Koch Energy Trading. It transferred the risks associated with a portfolio of 28 weather derivative contracts based on temperatures in 19 US cities.

In 2000-2001, the north-eastern US experienced a cold winter that resulted in a $5m loss of principal.

There was limited interest in using cat bonds to hedge temperature risk until the $31m Market Re bond that was sponsored by Allianz in 2016.

George Town Re (St Paul Re, 2001)

Issued in 1996, George Town Re was considered to be one of the first broadly distributed cat bonds, though today it might be classified as a sidecar. The debt and equity tranches totalled $68.5m. It covered most of the global property insurance business written by St Paul Re.

A series of events, including Hurricane Floyd and Windstorms Anatol, Lothar and Martin (all in 1999), flooding in the UK in 2000, and the World Trade Center bombing, pushed George Town Re into a loss of under $1m.

Nelson (Glacier, 2005)

Glacier Re was a short-lived, Swiss reinsurer. In June 2007 it issued Nelson Re – a $68m cat bond covering US hurricane, US earthquake and European windstorm risks. In 2010, Glacier was bought by Catalina Holdings to be run off. Catalina claimed $32m from Nelson.

After a protracted legal battle, Catalina withdrew its arbitration claim on behalf of Glacier Re and the principal was returned to investors in full in March 2013.

KAMP Re (Zurich 2005)

Just weeks after its launch, Swiss Re's $190m Kamp Re cat bond was hit by losses caused by Hurricane Katrina. The partial default meant that investors eventually received $46m.

Avalon Re (OIL Casualty, 2005)

Cayman Islands-domiciled Avalon Re was formed to protect Oil Casualty Insurance Ltd against insured casualty-related losses above $300m for three years from its inception in 2005.

Losses from the Buncefield oil depot explosion and a New York steam pipe explosion meant that the bond was impaired by $13m when it eventually matured.

Lehman Brothers

The Lehman collapse in the middle of the financial crisis had a direct impact on the catastrophe bond market. Four bonds defaulted due to capital losses on the collateral and the failure of the total return swap with Lehman. These losses paralysed the market for a time, though issuance eventually restarted with much tighter collateral provisions. In today's market both sponsors and investors usually insist that funds are invested in short-dated treasury money market funds.

- Ajax Re (Aspen, 2008)
- Carillon (Munich, 2008)
- Newton (Catlin, 2008)
- Willow (Allstate, 2008)

Muteki (Zenkyoren, 2011)

The Tohoku earthquake triggered Muteki, which was 10 weeks from its five-year maturity.

Immediately after the event, it was unclear whether Muteki, which was triggered by readings at seismic stations, would pay out as many of the stations were destroyed by the event. Eventually, there was no ambiguity about the payout. The $300m default is the largest so far.

Mariah Re (American Family, 2011)

In 2011 a heavy tornado season hit Kansas causing two cat bonds to default. This resulted in the loss of the full principal investment of $200m. Some investors filed a lawsuit based on an allegation that the reporting of catastrophe events was revised in order to allow American Family Mutual to call in the cat bonds.

According to the lawsuit, American Family colluded with service companies to inflate payouts from the cat bonds by altering reports of industry loss estimates. The case was dismissed in 2014.

Mexico MultiCat (FONDEN, 2015)

When it formed in the Pacific in October 2015, Hurricane Patricia was the second most intense tropical cyclone ever recorded anywhere in the world. It weakened rapidly before hitting a relatively uninhabited region on the western coast of Mexico.

The default for Mexico MultiCat Class C was triggered by landfall pressures that were interpolated from National Hurricane Center estimates that took over three months to publish.

It was not clear to the market how these estimates were made and there was considerable speculation on the secondary market. Eventually the bond paid out 50% of its $100m value.

Gator Re (American Family, 2016)

Gator Re is likely to pay out approximately $20m of the $200m principal to cover an accumulation of storm losses during 2016. Unusually, there was no franchise deductible (hurdle) to exclude losses from small events.

4.4 Drivers of catastrophe bond pricing

Cat bond prices have responded to at least three external factors – the broadening acceptance of the asset class; excess capacity in the reinsurance market and the price of risk in other asset classes. Returns are now at long-term lows.

Figure 8 shows the risk–return relationship for bonds issued in 2015 and 2016. There was little change in the pricing of bonds in those two years. Bonds with an expected loss of 2% paid a spread of about 5% above the floating rate.

Figure 9 plots the implied coupon spread for 2% expected losses at the first of every month back to January 1 2002 using the prior twelve months of cat bond issues at each date. This has been compared to an index of risk spread in the high-yield bond market and an index of US ILW prices.

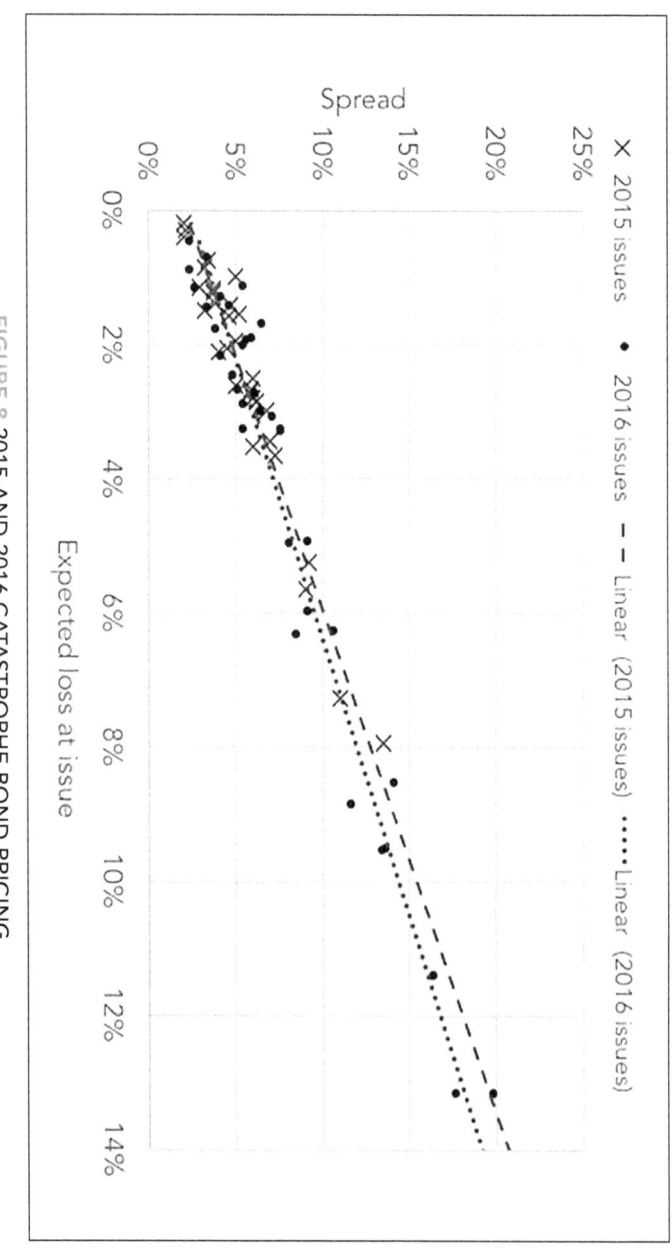

FIGURE 8 2015 AND 2016 CATASTROPHE BOND PRICING

Junk bond spread is BofA Merrill Lynch US High Yield Master II Option-Adjusted Spread© US $50bn (all perils) ILW is from Guy Carpenter. Both indices have been offset by 6 months so that the timings are consistent with the 12 month trailing average for cat bonds

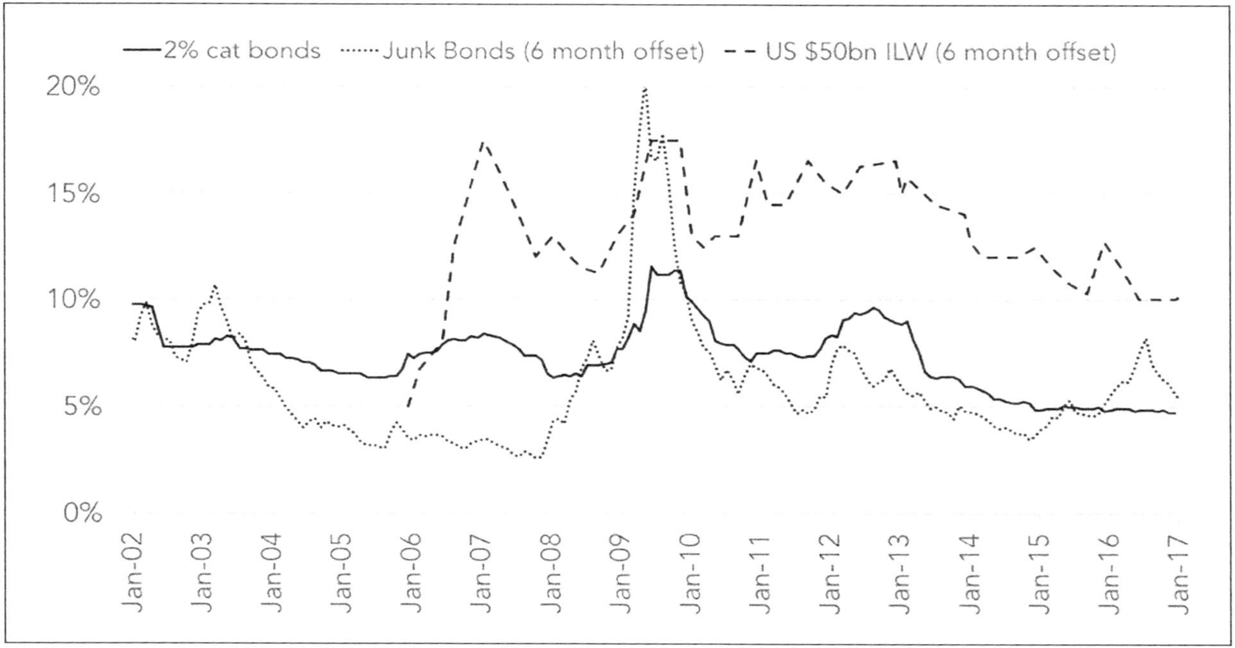

—— 2% cat bonds ·········· Junk Bonds (6 month offset) – – US $50bn ILW (6 month offset)

FIGURE 9 CHANGES IN CATASTROPHE BOND PRICING SINCE 2002

Factor 1. The perception of ILS has changed from an exotic asset class to something much more mainstream and this explains much of the secular decline in yields. This change in perception has meant a significant change in the types of investors that invest in cat bonds (or pay ILS funds to invest for them).

In 2002, cat bonds were largely owned by reinsurance companies and hedge funds. Today, institutional asset managers – including pension funds – are driving the market. These investors have much lower return thresholds.

Factor 2. Issuing cat bonds is an alternative to buying reinsurance which causes a correlation in the pricing of the two markets. The higher returns in 2006 and 2007 are likely to be related to hurricanes Katrina, Rita and Wilma in 2005 which had a dramatic effect on reinsurance pricing due to the sudden reduction in global reinsurance capital. Conversely, it seems likely that today's cat bond prices are affected by the surplus of capital in the reinsurance industry. The growth of the cat bond market has itself been part of the cause of the excess capital.

Factor 3. The other two jumps in spread – at the beginning of 2009 and 2012 – are harder to associate with loss events in the reinsurance market. But a plot of high junk bond yields shows similar movements, which suggests a third factor – the general widening of risk premiums caused by the global financial crisis and the Eurozone crisis. The high cat bond spreads in 2002 also corresponded to a peak in junk bond yields following the collapse of the dotcom bubble, although the 2016 spike in junk bond yields did not correspond with increased cat bond spreads.

Does this final factor undermine the non-correlation argument that is used to sell cat bonds in the first place? Not really – most of the volatility of cat bond returns is related to defaults rather than yields.

Author's note

Much has been written about the industry. News, analysis and links to other resources can be found at:

http://insurancelinked.com

Feedback and corrections are all gratefully received:

adam.alvarez@insurancelinked.com

Adam Alvarez
2017, London

About the author

Adam Alvarez is the Principal of InsuranceLinked, a consultancy that works at the intersection of the reinsurance and asset management industries. Clients have included Guy Carpenter, McKinsey and Nephila. His articles on the market have been syndicated by organisations such as Bloomberg, SNL and the magazine of the Australian Actuaries Institute.

Adam has been involved with insurance-linked securities since 2002 when he worked as a consultant at RMS designing the triggers for early parametric deals. He moved to Bermuda in 2005, where he helped to establish a new reinsurance platform within the Hiscox Group. During almost eight years at Hiscox, Adam managed the firm's ILS portfolio and a variety of other business lines. He has been based in London since 2016.

Adam has a degree in Physics from the University of Oxford and an MBA from INSEAD in France.